Grade One

Acoustic Guitar

Accompaniment

Compiled by

The Specialists in Guitar Education

RGT®

Registry of Guitar Tutors

www.RGT.org

Printed and bound in Great Britain

A CIP record for this publication is available from the British Library
ISBN: 978-1-905908-41-7

Published by Registry Publications

Registry Mews, Wilton Rd, Bexhill, Sussex, TN40 1HY

Text by Tony Skinner and Merv Young.
All musical compositions by Tony Skinner.
Design by JAK Images.
Front cover photo ©Smileus/Fotolia.
Rear cover photo ©ittipol/Fotolia.

Compiled by

v.20131118

Contents

CD track listing

Introduction

This book is designed primarily to provide supplementary learning materials for candidates preparing for the Accompaniment section of the Registry of Guitar Tutors (RGT) Grade One acoustic guitar playing exam. However, it should also prove helpful for anyone wishing to develop their accompaniment skills.

Accompaniment is an important skill for any guitarist and is particularly relevant for acoustic guitarists who want to accompany someone singing (be it themselves or another vocalist) or to accompany another instrumentalist.

In essence, the role of an accompanist is to bring two elements to the overall performance: rhythm and harmony. The chords themselves provide the harmony and the timing of how the chords are played provides the rhythm. In this book the focus is predominantly on the rhythmic elements, as this is where the main decisions are to be made at this level of playing. You will, however, find fretboxes, showing the recommended fingering for all the chords required for the Grade One exam in the Chord Shapes chapter on pages 19 and 20.

This book contains 10 different melodies that have been notated, along with the appropriate chord chart for each one. There are also some tips with each example to get you thinking about how to approach developing your own rhythm playing ideas.

There is also a CD with this book that contains each melody being played on two different tracks. The first CD track for each melody features a guitar playing an example chord accompaniment along with the melody (played twice). The second CD track features the melody on its own (played three times), so that you can play the chords and practise your own accompaniment skills.

Exam Format

In the accompaniment section of the RGT acoustic guitar exams, the candidate is required to play a chordal accompaniment while the examiner plays an eight-bar melody.

In the exam, the candidate will be shown a chord chart for the melody. The examiner will then give a one bar count-in and play the melody once, just for the candidate to listen to without playing along. The examiner will then give another one bar count-in and the melody will be played a further three times without stopping. The candidate can accompany the first of these three verses if they wish to, but only the accompaniment of the second and third verses will be assessed.

Frequently Asked Questions:

Q: In the exam, will I be shown the notation for the melody?

A: No. The melody notation played by the examiner will not be seen by the candidate. This way the candidate can focus on the chord chart and using their musical and aural abilities to create the most appropriate accompaniment.

Q: How will the examiner play the melody?

A: The examiner will play the melody either live on a guitar or keyboard, or via a recording.

Q: Will the examiner give me any advice on how to play the accompaniment?

A: No. The main purpose of this section of the exam is to assess your ability to make musical decisions about the most appropriate way to perform the chords that are presented to you.

Q: Will the examiner let me know when I am supposed to start my playing?

A: The examiner will 'cue you in', although the method of doing so may vary according to the melody being played. As part of your practice with this book, work on being able to follow the chord charts so that you know exactly when to come in by yourself.

Q: Will the examiner require me to use the same fingerings for the chord shapes that are shown in this book or in the exam handbook?

A: No. Any alternative chord fingerings will be acceptable, provided the chord itself is musically correct.

Accompaniment Advice

In the exam, the style of the accompaniment is left to the candidate's discretion, and the candidate can chose to either strum or fingerpick. The CD demo recordings that are provided with this book are intended to give an indication of the technical level that would be expected for a very high mark at this grade. (Note that only the two assessed verses are provided in each accompaniment demo recording.) To ensure that you can clearly hear the accompaniment guitar part on the CD demo tracks, the level of the accompaniment guitar has deliberately been made louder than would normally occur in a standard recording. The demo recordings of the accompaniment parts are not intended to provide exact templates for candidates to copy; they are provided as examples of the standard required, and candidates are strongly encouraged to devise their own rhythmic/picking styles.

The demo recordings also provide an insight into the factors that need to be considered when developing accompaniment ideas. When accompanying, each melody can be interpreted in a number of ways and there will be a range of playing techniques and rhythm styles that can be effectively adopted. The essence of this book is to enable the player to start developing their playing skills so that sympathetic musical decisions can be made to both support and enhance the melody being played.

In general, it will be possible for the chords to be played in a range of styles including: strumming using a combination of down and up strokes; using simple arpeggiated patterns with either the fingers or a plectrum (pick); using a specific musical playing style, such as a continuous downstroke strumming pattern.

Accompaniment Tips

1. Your playing should always relate to the timing and style of the melody played by the examiner.

2. Remember that the very first time the examiner plays the melody, you have the opportunity to listen to it without needing to play along. Use this opportunity to listen carefully and try to absorb the melodic shape and structure of the melody.

3. In the first verse of the three continuous playings your playing will not be assessed, so you can best use this time by reading through the chord chart and just strumming once on the first beat of each bar so that the timing becomes clearly fixed in your mind.

4. In the remaining two verses use an appropriate rhythm or picking style that suits the mood, style and timing of the melody. When you are practising the examples in this book, keep experimenting to develop your own musical ideas. Try to listen to any rhythmic elements of the melody that you can respond to and emulate with the chords.

5. Keep listening closely to the melody while playing your accompaniment and make sure to keep in time with it. The ability to stay in time with the melody is one of the most important aspects of accompaniment. In the exam itself, and when practising, try to ensure that your chord changes come in clearly on the first beat of each bar, to help establish a definite pulse and rhythm.

6. Ensure that you are totally comfortable with playing all the chord shapes on their own before you attempt them with the accompaniment practice track.

7. Use your knowledge of the chord shapes to change smoothly from one chord to another, whilst making sure your chords ring clear. It might be that the strumming is fluent but the chord changes are not as smooth as they need to be. In that case, initially try playing along with one of the example melodies but just strumming each chord once – this will allow you more time to change to the next chord. (Remember that this advice is only for practising the chord changes, not how to play in the exam itself.)

8. Take time to listen to how the chords themselves sound. It is very easy to get so wrapped up in the fingering and chord shapes that you don't listen carefully to the sound you are producing. Are all the strings ringing out clearly? Is there buzzing from any of the fretted notes? If so, check that the fretting fingers are pressing with their tips and are as close to the frets as possible.

9. Try to include some simple variation in the final verse if possible. At this level this needn't be too complicated, but try to develop your strumming pattern ideas slightly as you are playing with the practice tracks. The more you practise this, the more instinctive this ability will become.

10. If you make a mistake whilst playing the accompaniment, DO NOT STOP. It is important for the overall musical result that you keep playing (something – anything!) so that you do not lose your place in the music and fall out of time with the melody. Regardless of what mistake you might make with a chord shape, it will never sound worse than if you come to a complete stop – particularly as the melody will carry on without you. If you cannot change to a chord in time, then simply place your fretting hand across the strings to mute them whilst you carry on strumming – it's not ideal, but it will definitely sound preferable to a total halt and the risk of losing your co-ordination with the melody.

Chord Charts

Examples of the type of chord charts that will occur in the Accompaniment section of the RGT acoustic guitar playing exam are given on the following pages. Note that these chord charts are provided only as examples of *the types* of chord charts that may occur in the exam.

Below each example chord chart in this chapter, the melody, that it is designed to accompany, is provided in both standard notation and tablature. Note that in the exam itself, the melody will NOT be shown to the candidate; it is provided in this book purely for situations where a teacher might wish to play the melody with a student rather than use the CD provided. To avoid any chance of confusion, we reiterate that the melody notation will NOT be provided in the exam itself.

A sample rhythm pattern has been notated below each chord chart in this chapter; this is the rhythm pattern that is used on the demonstration track. It provides an example of the standard expected for this grade. Each rhythm pattern has been designed to reflect some of the main rhythmic features of the melody. The rhythm pattern can be used as a starting point for your own rhythm playing. However, for each chord chart, this will be just one of many different interpretations that are possible and you are encouraged to explore and practise different rhythm patterns, so as to develop your rhythm playing technique and your ability to reflect the main rhythmic elements of a melody.

For each example on the following pages there are some specific tips and advice that are relevant to that chord chart and melody. Use these as ideas from which to start developing your own interpretations. The advice is intended to help you to develop your own skills and confidence in this area of playing, so keep practising and experimenting.

At this grade, all the chord charts will be in $^4_4$ time, and the range of chords will be restricted to those listed below:

A C D E G   Am Dm Em   A7 B7 D7 E7

Fretboxes showing the fingering for all these chords are provided at the back of this book.

There will be three *different* chords in each chord chart. There will be two bars of each chord, apart from the very final bar (after the repeat), in which the final chord should be played with a single strum.

Chord Chart 1 (CD Track 1)

On the demonstration track the chords are played with the following rhythm:

This pattern draws on the main rhythmic features of the melody – i.e. the two eighth notes that are played on beat 3 of the melody in the first 6 bars. The fairly slow tempo of this melody makes a strumming pattern of Down Down DownUpDown particularly effective, as it reflects the smooth and relaxed feel of the melody. This rhythm is adopted on the demonstration track, with the upstroke playing the eighth note that occurs after beat 3 of the pattern.

The final two bars of the melody consist of quarter notes only. Your rhythm playing could simply emulate that, or as a contrast you could try playing the rhythm pattern above with downstrokes only in bars 7 and 8. Alternatively, try experimenting with some different rhythm patterns for these two bars, or for the last bar alone, to help create a contrasting musical feel before the melody repeats. On the demonstration track, in the second playing, you can hear a contrasting pattern in bar 8.

Melody 1 (CD Track 2)

Chord Chart 2 (CD Track 3)

On the demonstration track the chords are played with the following rhythm:

This pattern draws on some of the main rhythmic features of the melody, particularly the two eighth notes that are played on beat 2 of the melody in several bars. There are various ways the rhythm pattern could be strummed. On the demonstration track the eighth note that occurs after beat 2 of the pattern is played with an upstroke, whilst all the main beats are played with downstrokes. However, to maintain a smooth strumming pattern you could try using a combination of downstrokes and upstrokes (Down DownUpDown Up). Alternatively, to give the rhythm more energy, you might like to try strumming this pattern using only downstrokes.

As you get familiar with this chord chart, try to vary the rhythm pattern a little over certain bars. For instance, bars 4 and 8 of the melody both contain fewer notes so your rhythm playing could emulate that, or alternatively try a busier rhythm as a contrast (as played on the demonstration track during the second play through).

Melody 2 (CD Track 4)

Chord Chart 3 (CD Track 5)

On the demonstration track the chords are played with the following rhythm:

Sometimes a simple strumming pattern can be the most effective rhythm style to use, especially where the melody itself has a relatively straightforward rhythm. On the demonstration track all downstrokes were used during the first playing. So you just need to relax your strumming hand and focus on playing the chords accurately and smoothly on every beat of each bar. Of course, there is some variety to the melody in bars 2, 4 and 8 so you could experiment on those bars with some different strumming ideas. For instance, in bars 4 and 8, in order to provide some rhythmic uplift at the end of these melodic phrases, you might like to try playing the following pattern which you can hear on the demonstration track:

Melody 3 (CD Track 6)

Chord Chart 4 (CD Track 7)

| **4/4** :∥ **D** | **D** | **E**m | **E**m | |

| **D** | **D** | **A7** | **A7** :∥ **D** | ∥ |

On the demonstration track the chords are played with the following rhythm:

The strumming pattern reflects the main rhythmic features of the melody – i.e. the two eighth notes that are played on beat 2 of the melody during four of the bars. Although this rhythm pattern is played throughout on the demonstration track the rhythm of the melody does feature some variety, so you might like to try experimenting with some different patterns to reflect the way the rhythm of the melody changes. For instance, a busier rhythm pattern in the fourth bar might provide an effective contrast, perhaps with eighth notes played over beats 3 and 4 as played on the demonstration track during the second time through.

The faster tempo of this melody means that the use of downstrokes might be more effective to help create and maintain a lively feel throughout the performance. You can hear what this sounds like on the demonstration track where downstrokes are used throughout. Also, experiment by playing the notated pattern using a combination of downstrokes and upstrokes, to see which you prefer the sound of.

Melody 4 (CD Track 8)

Chord Chart 5 (CD Track 9)

$\frac{4}{4}$ ‖: **E**m		**E**m		**D**		**D**	

| **A**m | | **A**m | | **D** | | **D** | :‖ **E**m | | |

On the demonstration track you'll notice that the chords are played using a fingerstyle pattern, rather than being strummed. The fretting hand is holding down the relevant chord shape in each bar and the picking hand is playing a steady eighth note pattern. The bass note of each chord is played first with the thumb, followed by strings 1, 2 and 3 using three different fingers with the picking hand:

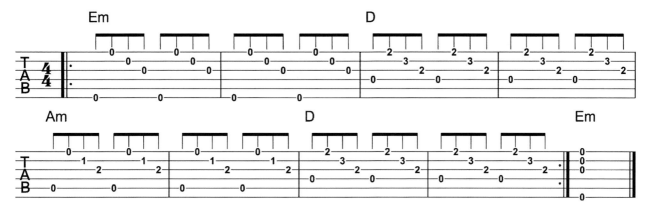

You don't have to use your fingers to play this pattern; the same effect can be produced by using a pick (plectrum) to play each individual note in the chord. Either way, fret the entire chord shape, even if you aren't intending to play those notes in your fingerstyle pattern – that way you'll be still playing notes from the chord if your picking hand accidently strikes a different string from the pattern you intended.

Melody 5 (CD Track 10)

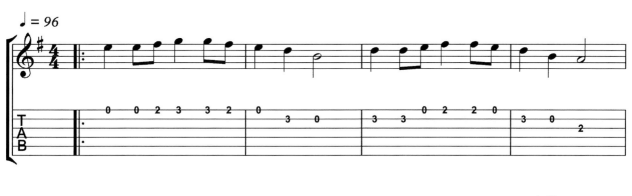

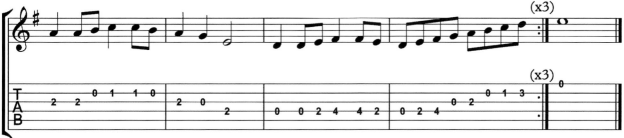

13

Chord Chart 6 (CD Track 11)

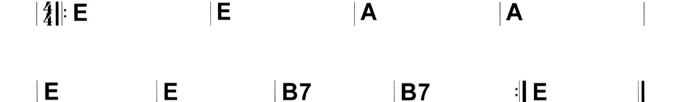

On the demonstration track the chords are played with the following rhythm:

In this example, a fairly straightforward strumming pattern has been adopted and is played using downstrokes throughout. The melody is played at a fairly fast tempo and features a variety of different rhythms. The use of a simpler rhythm pattern can be very effective in these instances as it can act as both a contrast to the melody, as well as giving the melody some space so that the overall performance doesn't sound too cluttered.

You should experiment to hear the effect of playing busier rhythm patterns in some bars. For example, you could play two eighth note strums (DownUp) at the start of bars 2 and 6, as a contrast to the four quarter notes that appear in the melody in those bars – you can hear this on the demonstration track during the second play through.

Melody 6 (CD Track 12)

Chord Chart 7 (CD Track 13)

On the demonstration track the chords are played with the following rhythm:

The melody for this example uses the same rhythm for the first 7 bars. The essence of this rhythm is reflected in the strumming pattern that is used on the demonstration track, although the final beat of the bar contains a quarter note strum rather than exactly copying the two eighth notes that appear at the end of each bar in the melody. As well as providing some space for the melody notes on the final beat, this approach also gives you a little more time to change onto the next chord – always an important consideration if you are to maintain a smooth and fluent rhythmic feel.

On the demonstration track this pattern is played using downstrokes and upstrokes as follows: Down Down DownUpDown, with the upstroke being played on the second eighth note just after the third beat. As with the other examples, experiment with different combinations of downstrokes and upstrokes, as well as busier or simpler rhythms, to reflect and enhance the repetitive riff-based nature of this melody. On the demonstration track bars 4 and 8 feature some rhythmic variation during the repeat playing.

Melody 7 (CD Track 14)

Chord Chart 8 (CD Track 15)

| $\frac{4}{4}$ ‖: **D**m | | | **D**m | | **C** | | **C** | |

| **D**m | **D**m | **A**m | **A**m :‖ **D**m | ‖

On the demonstration track the chords are played with the following rhythm:

The main rhythmic feature that occurs in several bars of the melody is used here with the eighth notes being played on beat 2. On the demonstration track the second of these eighth notes is played with an upstroke (Down DownUpDown Down). However, the faster tempo of this melody means that the use of downstrokes throughout might also be effective. Alternatively, you might prefer playing the pattern using downstrokes in certain bars only – such as bars 4 and 8. You can hear some variation to the rhythm in these bars on the demonstration track played using downstrokes and upstrokes. Try experimenting further by playing these variations (or your own) with downstrokes only.

When deciding whether to use downstrokes or upstrokes there is often no correct or incorrect approach; they will just sound slightly different and impart a different musical feel to the performance. You should experiment to see what is comfortable to you as a player, and listen carefully to hear how the different approaches fit with the melody.

Melody 8 (CD Track 16)

$\quad \downarrow = 138$

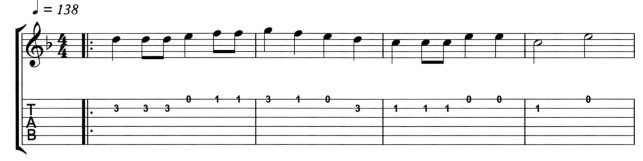

Chord Chart 9 (CD Track 17)

| $\frac{4}{4}$‖: A7 | A7 | D7 | D7 | |
| A7 | A7 | E | E | :‖ A7 ‖ |

On the demonstration track the chords are played with the following rhythm:

♩ ♩ ♩ ♫

Sometimes a melody with a repetitive rhythm can be effectively accompanied by replicating the rhythm almost exactly. This approach has been adopted on the demonstration track here, with the strumming pattern being played with downstrokes throughout to help drive the riff-based melody along in this mid-tempo piece.

Bar 8 of the melody contains a different rhythm so you might want to try a different strumming pattern here, or perhaps vary the combination of downstrokes and upstrokes in this bar. You can hear a variation to the strumming pattern on the demonstration track during the second play through.

As the final strum is on the eighth note that occurs just after beat 4, take care with your chord changes in this example to make sure you shift onto the next chord fluently and clearly.

Melody 9 (CD Track 18)

♩ = 106

Chord Chart 10 (CD Track 19)

E7	E7	A7	A7

B7	B7	E7	E7	E7

On the demonstration track the chords are played with the following rhythm:

The rhythm pattern here reflects the main rhythmic elements of the melody – i.e. the four eighth notes that start each bar. On the demonstration track these eighth notes are played using downstrokes and upstrokes, with the final two quarter notes played as downstrokes: DownUpDownUpDown Down. You might prefer the harder-edged sound that strumming this pattern using all downstrokes throughout creates, so try that approach as well.

In bars 2, 4, 6 and 8 of the melody the final note is allowed to ring on into beats 3 and 4. It can be effective in these instances to have a chord being strummed whilst this melody note rings out to provide extra interest to the overall performance. This is the reason for the two quarter note strums on beats 3 and 4 in the demonstration track. However, experiment here to try some other rhythms and explore some alternative approaches that could also be effective. For instance, the demonstration track features some different strumming ideas during the repeat playing in bars 4 and 8.

Melody 10 (CD Track 20)

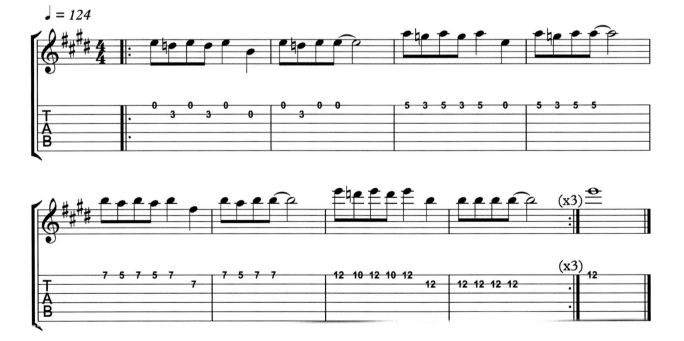

Chord Shapes

Below is the fingering for the full range of chords that may occur in the Accompaniment section of the Grade One RGT acoustic guitar playing exam.

If, in the exam, you prefer to use an alternative fingering for any chord, that would be perfectly acceptable, providing that the pitches are all accurate and an effective musical result is produced.

Tip:

It may be easier to remember chord shapes if you bear in mind that fingerings for chord shapes with the same root note are sometimes just variations of the major chord shape. For example: Em is the same as E major but with the first finger omitted from the fingering, and E7 is the same as E major but with the 3rd finger omitted from the fingering.

Also, try to identify and remember similarities between different chords. For example, Am is very similar to C major – only the third finger needs to move to change between these chords.

A   C   D

E

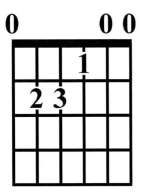

G

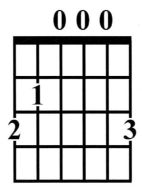

Am

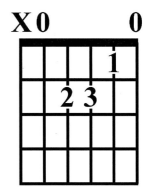

Dm

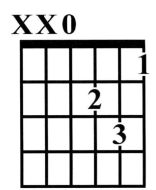

Em

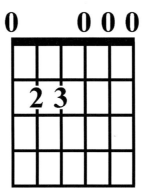

A7

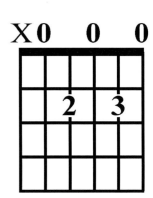

B7

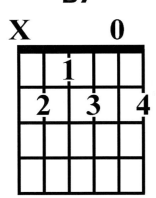

D7

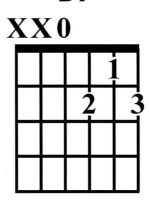

E7

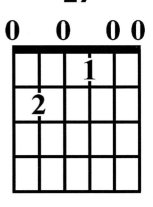